Water

Andrew Charman

W
FRANKLIN WATTS
LONDON•SYDNEY

This edition 2003

Franklin Watts
96 Leonard Street
London EC2A 4XD

Franklin Watts Australia
45-51 Huntley Street
Alexandria
NSW 2015

Series editor: Pippa Pollard
Editor: Claire Llewellyn
Design: Shaun Barlow
Artwork: Alec Hitchins
Picture research: Ambreen Husain

Educational advisor:
Joy Richardson

A CIP catalogue record for
this book is available from the
British Library

ISBN 0 7496 5068 0

Printed in Italy

Contents

The watery planet

From space you can see that very large areas of planet Earth are covered with water. Most of it is in the seas and oceans. This is salty water which land animals cannot drink. Luckily, there is also a lot of fresh water. This is in lakes, rivers, ponds and in the ground. Animals and plants need this water. They cannot live without it.

▽ The seas and oceans cover more of Earth's surface than the land.

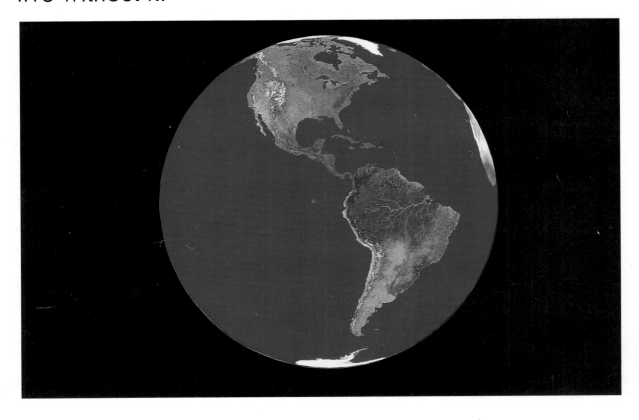

What is water?

Most things on Earth are solid, liquid or a gas. Water can be all three. When water gets very cold it becomes a solid, called ice. Hot water becomes **water vapour**, which is a gas. Usually, water is a liquid. When water is liquid it is a very good **solvent**. This means that other substances mix with it easily.

▷ It is as a liquid that water is most useful to the plants and animals that live on Earth.

▷ Water vapour rises into the air and cools. It changes into droplets of water which make clouds or low-lying fog.

▷ Mountain tops are very cold places. Some are covered with snow and ice.

The water cycle

There is always the same amount of water on Earth. It moves around the planet in a never-ending cycle. Water falls to the ground as rain. It then flows to the sea along rivers and streams. The Sun heats the sea. Water rises into the air as a gas called water vapour. The vapour cools and makes bigger droplets. These fall to Earth as rain.

▷ Clouds contain droplets of water. A cloud 'bursts' when the droplets become too heavy. They fall as rain.

▷ Rainwater drains off the land into rivers and streams. These flow to the sea.

Water for life

Our bodies are mostly water. Inside us, the **chemicals** which keep us alive are mixed with water. **Blood** moves these chemicals around our bodies. It, too, is mostly water.

Our bodies lose water when we breathe, sweat and go to the toilet. This water must be replaced. We cannot live long without water.

▷ Water on our skin cools us. This is why we sweat when we are very active.

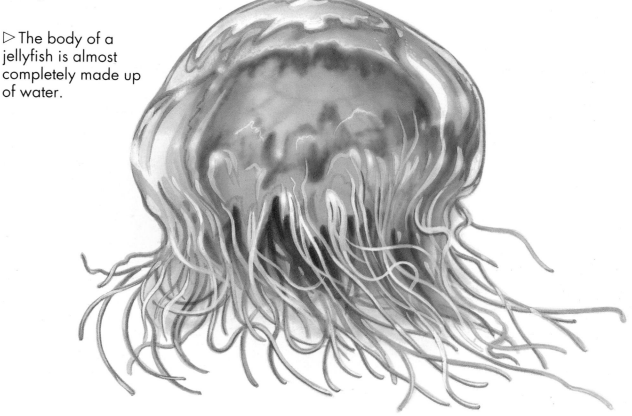

▷ The body of a jellyfish is almost completely made up of water.

▷ We need to drink to replace the water that is lost from our bodies.

Plants and water

Plants are able to make food for themselves in their leaves. To do this they need a gas called **carbon dioxide** from the air, and water from the soil. They also need sunlight. Plants soak up water through their roots. The food they make in the leaves travels around the plant in the **sap**. This sap, like an animal's blood, is mostly water.

▽ Some plants store water. This stops them from drying out.

◁ The roots of plants grow into the soil and soak up water. Roots are usually hidden underground. Here, the soil has been washed away and the roots can be seen.

▷ Mangrove trees grow in the tropics, where a river meets the sea. Their stilt roots support them in the soft, wet mud.

Life in the sea

Water flows to the sea from the land. It contains many **mineral salts**. As the sea is warmed by the Sun, water vapour rises, but the salts remain. This makes the sea salty. The smallest plants and animals in the sea are called **plankton**. They float in the water and are food for many of the animals that live there.

▽ This is what plankton looks like through a microscope.

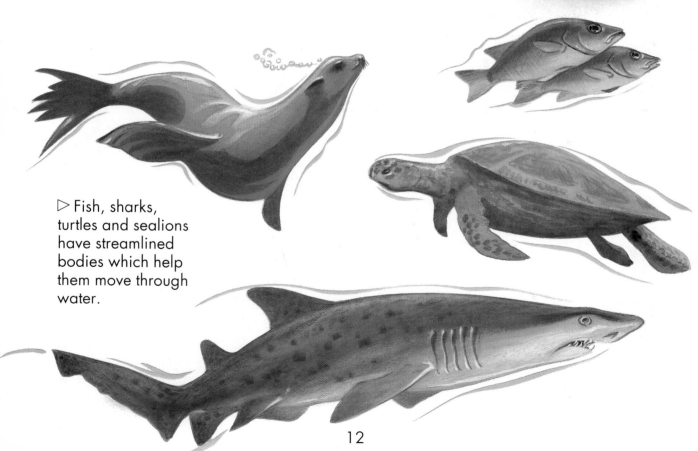

▷ Fish, sharks, turtles and sealions have streamlined bodies which help them move through water.

12

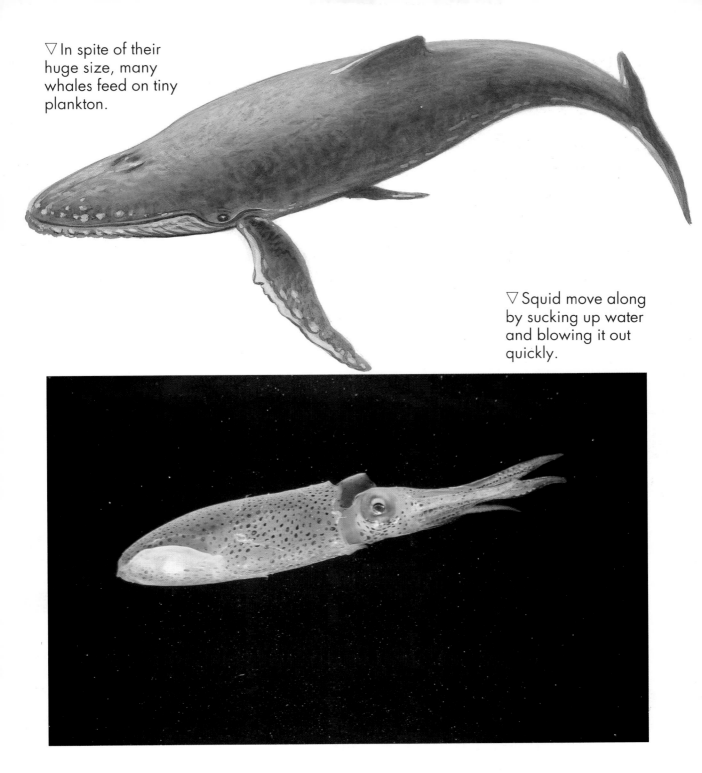

▽ In spite of their huge size, many whales feed on tiny plankton.

▽ Squid move along by sucking up water and blowing it out quickly.

Life in fresh water

Rainwater does not contain salts like the sea. It is called fresh water, and is good to drink. On land, rainwater flows into streams and rivers. The soil may soak it up, or it may collect in lakes and ponds. Few creatures can live in water which flows very quickly. Where it slows down, plants can grow and animals live among them.

▽ Most salmon live in salt water. They return to their home rivers to lay their eggs.

▷ Water flows downhill to the sea. A waterfall is a sudden drop from a high place in a river or stream.

▽ The still waters of ponds are home to many different kinds of plants and animals.

Dragonfly

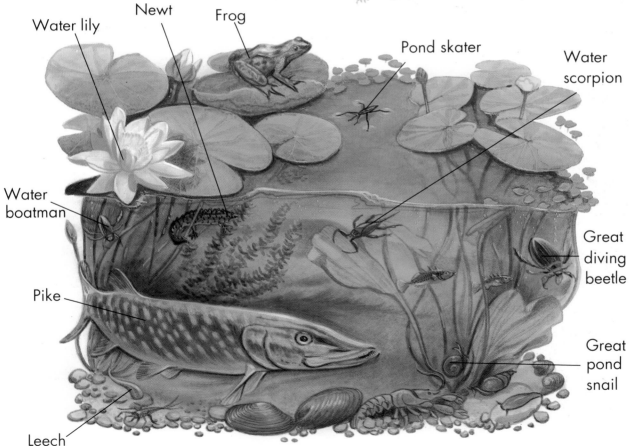

Water lily

Newt

Frog

Pond skater

Water scorpion

Water boatman

Great diving beetle

Pike

Great pond snail

Leech

Ice

Water freezes at a temperature of 0° **Centigrade**. When the air is cold, snow falls from the clouds. In very cold places it never melts. This happens on high mountain peaks and at the North and South Pole. Plants cannot grow here. They cannot take frozen water up into their leaves. Few animals can survive the bitter cold.

▷ An iceberg is a chunk of ice which has broken away from the pack ice. It will float until it melts.

△ Polar bears live near the North Pole. Their fur and a thick layer of body fat keep them warm.

◁Keeping warm at the South Pole. Penguins have a thick layer of feathers. Seals have a layer of body fat.

△Lichens are able to grow where it is too cold for other plants. They do not have roots.

Life without water

Deserts are places where rain rarely falls. There is very little water in the ground. The huge areas of ice at the **Poles** are deserts. Other kinds of desert are baking hot. They are huge areas of dry rock and gravel or sand dunes. The plants and animals that live in hot deserts can survive on small amounts of water for a long time.

▷ A camel can hold a lot of water in its stomach. These camels live in the Sahara desert in North Africa.

▷ Desert rains fall suddenly and then are gone. The Saguaro cactus can store huge amounts of water in its stem.

▽ Desert animals
need to keep cool.
The gerboa stays in
its burrow during the
heat of the day.

19

Water changes things

Water is a powerful force. Over many years it can break down large rocks into small pieces. Fast-flowing rivers carve deep valleys. The sea crashes against the land and slowly wears it away.

At the mouth of a river, the opposite happens. Mud in the water drops to the river bed and piles up, making new land. This is called **silting**.

▷ Fast-moving rivers break down rocks and carry the soil away.

▽ A river slows down as it reaches the sea. The mud it is carrying sinks to the bottom and makes new land.

▽ The power of waves slowly wears away the softer rocks along the coast. This forms remarkable shapes.

J137,289

Floating and sinking

Some things float in water, others sink. A substance floats when it is less dense than water. This means that an amount of the substance is lighter than the same amount of water. Air is less dense than water. Things which are filled with air will float. Substances will sink if they are denser than water. Stone is denser than water and will sink.

▽ Even a ship as large as this one will float while it has plenty of air inside it. If it is overloaded, however, it will sink.

▽ Ice is less dense than water, but not by much. An iceberg will float, but most of it is underwater.

◁ Submarines contain tanks which are filled with air. The submarine goes down when the tanks are filled with water.

23

Water supply

People need water to drink and to grow their **crops.** In some very hot countries, people have to walk a long way to collect water from a well. They may carry it to the fields to water dry crops. This is called **irrigation**.

In other countries, rainwater is stored in **reservoirs**. It is cleaned and then piped to people's homes.

▷ Wells are built to reach water under the ground. Collecting water is tiring and it can take many hours.

▽ A reservoir looks like a lake, but it is man-made. It is used for storing water.

▽ In dry areas, water from wells may be pumped through pipes and canals to irrigate the crops.

Using water

We use water in many different ways. People have sailed boats on water since the earliest times. Moving water has **energy**. It can be used to turn wheels for grinding grain or making electricity. Water can also be used to cool machinery. In most cars, water is used to cool the engine. Water is also used to wash things.

▷ There are many different water sports. This person is surfing.

◁ Flowing water has the energy to turn a wheel. The wheel may move machinery to grind grain.

▽ We use water to wash and to keep things clean.

Looking after water

All living things need clean water, yet it can easily become **polluted.** This happens when harmful substances are mixed with it. The **chemicals** which are used in factories and by farmers can pollute our water. So can the **sewage** from toilets. Plants and animals cannot live in very polluted water. We need to protect clean water, and not waste it.

▷ This water has been cleaned. It is safe to put back into the swamp.

▷ This river has been polluted with chemicals. Many of the plants and animals have died.

▽ An oil-tanker
accident at sea may
cause an oil spill.
The oil is very
harmful to wildlife.

Things to do

- Make a study of the different kinds of water in your area. Are there ponds, lakes and rivers? Look at the same area on a map. Can you see where rivers join up? How far away is the sea?

- Experiment with boats made out of different materials. Can you make a boat that floats out of a lump of modelling material? What happens to a floating egg box if you fill one side with stones? What does this tell you about how boats are loaded?

- How many different uses of water can you discover? You might like to find pictures of as many uses as you can and make a display.

Glossary

Blood The substance in our bodies which carries chemicals from one part to another.

Carbon dioxide A gas in air that plants use to make food. Animals breathe out carbon dioxide.

Centigrade A scale to measure how hot or cold something is. Water freezes at 0°C and boils at 100°C.

Chemicals Everything is made of chemicals. Some chemicals are harmful to plants and animals.

Crops The plants people grow for food, such as wheat and potatoes.

Energy The ability to do work. Moving water has energy.

Irrigation Taking water from one place to another so that it can be used to grow crops.

Mineral salts Some of the tiny pieces of rock and other substances which are washed off the land into the sea.

Plankton Tiny plants and animals which float in the sea.

Poles The frozen areas of land at the far North (the North Pole) and the far South (the South Pole) of the earth.

Polluted Spoilt by harmful substances.

Reservoir A place where a large amount of water is stored.

Sap The liquid substance inside plants that carries chemicals from one part to another.

Sewage Human waste from toilets.

Silting When tiny particles of rock and soil collect at the bottom of a river.

Solvent A substance which will mix easily with other substances.

Temperature How hot or cold something is.

Water vapour When water mixes with air it makes a gas called water vapour.

Index

Photographic credits:
A.N.T./NHPA 17, 27; Bruce Coleman Limited 14; Ecoscene 29; Chris Fairclough Colour Library 9; Robert Harding Picture Library 5; Hutchison Library 25; Trevor McDonald/ NHPA 10; Okapia/Oxford Scientific Films 21; Tom Van Sant/Geosphere Project, Santa Monica/Science Photo Library 3; Zefa Picture Library 7, 13, 19, 22.